"Justin and Lindsey have written a book to help us protect our children from sexual abuse. In clear and simple language, it engages the child in the discussion. Woven throughout is the foundational belief that our children have been purposefully created by God and that every aspect of their being was his idea. I highly recommend *God Made All of Me* to parents of young children. Love them well by educating them about keeping their bodies safe."

Diane Langberg, PhD, Psychologist and author of *Suffering and the Heart of God*

"This is a strange and beautiful book. Strange because it's so unique: exploring God's creation with a view to helping children protect themselves in an increasingly at-risk culture. Beautiful because it hits its mark: instilling practical wisdom in a way that teaches without terrifying. The combined experience of the authors makes this a terrific resource for parents as well. As a father of four, I highly recommend it."

Michael Horton, Professor of Systematic Theology and Apologetics, Westminster Seminary California

"A lively, engaging, and straightforward little book, *God Made All of Me* is the perfect invitation to start a conversation with children about their bodies, boundaries, and the people in their life that make them feel safe. This book is both God-glorifying and visually stimulating and our homes and churches will be safer and more joyful places because of it."

Rachel Held Evans, Blogger and author of *Faith Unraveled* and *Searching for Sunday*

"*God Made All of Me* is a sweet, compelling, brilliantly sensitive invitation to teach your children the beauty of their body and the honor due to being made in the image of God. It offers simple and clear wisdom that little ones can grasp about how to protect themselves from inappropriate or unwanted touch. It is the responsibility of every parent and grandparent to address uncomfortable subjects. This glorious resource is an investment in care, protection, and honor. I am grateful I get to read this to all three of my grandchildren."

Dan B. Allender, Professor of Counseling Psychology and Founding President, The Seattle School of Theology and Psychology; author of *The Wounded Heart* and *Healing the Wounded Heart*

"I wish my family had this book when I was a little girl, because if they did I wouldn't have the sexual abuse story I have today. This is an important, straightforward book."

Mary DeMuth, Author of *Not Marked: Finding Hope and Healing After Sexual Abuse*

"As a parent to a young daughter, I'm already thinking through how to parent well in this area. Too many resources, when I was growing up, made us feel shame because of our bodies, or just simply didn't talk about it. I'm so thankful and completely indebted to Justin and Lindsey for giving us a resource like this."

Jefferson Bethke, Author of *New York Times* best seller *Jesus > Religion*

"This is a must-read for any parent who wants to help empower their child to be safe from those who hurt little ones."

Michael Reagan, President, The Reagan Legacy Foundation

"This book is an absolute gift to parents! Finally, there is a quality book that engages children while providing a way for parents to discuss the difficult topic of sexual abuse. This is a vital tool to help parents raise healthy, brave children."

Lindsey Strickland, Former child advocate at Sexual Assault Resource Agency, Charlottesville, VA

"It's sad that we have to educate our children in self-protection; but it is profoundly necessary. The good news is we can rejoice that we are God's creation and teach our children to live in that sacred dignity. This book is a great help!"

Gregory O. Brewer, Bishop of the Episcopal Diocese of Central Florida

"Educating our children about their bodies is one of the most important steps in preventing child abuse. That's why *God Made All of Me* is a valuable resource. A simple story with colorful artwork, and theological and practical truth— all packed into one small book. Parents, educators, Sunday school teachers, children's ministry directors, and many others should pick up a copy today and read it to their young children."

Deepak Reju, Pastor of Biblical Counseling and Family Ministry, Capitol Hill Baptist Church (Washington, DC); and author of *On Guard: Preventing and Responding to Child Abuse at Church* and *The Pastor and Counseling*

GOD MADE

ALL

OF ME

A Book to Help Children Protect Their Bodies

Justin S. Holcomb &
Lindsey A. Holcomb

Illustrated
by Trish Mahoney

New Growth Press, Greensboro, NC 27404
Text Copyright © 2015 by Justin S. Holcomb and Lindsey A. Holcomb
Illustration Copyright © 2015 by Trish Mahoney

Art and Design: Trish Mahoney

ISBN: 978-1-942572-30-5 (Print)
ISBN: 978-1-942572-55-8 (eBook)

Library of Congress Cataloging-in-Publication Data
Holcomb, Justin S., 1973-
God made all of me : a book to help children protect their bodies /
authors, Justin S. Holcomb and Lindsey A. Holcomb.
pages cm
ISBN 978-1-942572-30-5 (print) -- ISBN 978-1-942572-55-8 (ebook)
1. Human body--Biblical teaching. 2. Human body--Religious
aspects--Christianity. 3. Child sexual abuse--Prevention. I. Holcomb,
Lindsey A., 1981- II. Title.
BS680.B6H65 2015
248.8'2--dc23

                              2015011669

Printed in Mexico

23 22 21 20 19 18 17 16   3 4 5 6 7

This book is dedicated to GRACE and all it does to empower and train Christian communities to recognize, prevent, and respond to child abuse.

Dear Parent or Caregiver,

Thank you for reading *God Made All of Me* to your child.

We wrote this book as a tool so you can explain to your children that God made their bodies. Because private parts are private, there can be lots of questions, curiosity, or shame regarding them. For their protection, children need to know about private parts and understand that God made their body and made it special.

The message children need to hear is: "God made all of you. Every part of your body is good, and some parts are private. He made the parts of your body that other people see every day, and he made your private parts. Every part is good because God made every part and called them all good."

Our goal is to help you in protecting your child from sexual abuse. We wrote *Rid of My Disgrace: Hope and Healing for Victims of Sexual Assault* because it is an important and prevalent issue. One in four women and one in six men have been or will be assaulted in their lifetime. Heartbreakingly, many of the victims of this epidemic are children: 15% of those assaulted are under age 12, and 29% are between ages 12 and 17. Girls between the ages of 16 and 19 are four times more likely than the general population to be victims of sexual assault.[*]

We want parents and caregivers to be smarter and better prepared than those who would want to harm the child they love and want to protect. While we know that actions by adults can be more effective than expecting children to protect themselves from sexual abuse, children still need accurate, age-appropriate information about child sexual abuse and confidence their parents and caregivers will support them.

Education is important in preventing inappropriate sexual behavior or contact. By teaching children about their bodies and discussing appropriate and inappropriate touch, you are helping them understand their ability to say No to unwanted touch, which will help them if anyone ever tries to hurt or trick them.

Thank you for taking the time to read this book and talk to your child about it.

Best,
Lindsey Holcomb, MPH
Justin Holcomb, PhD

[*] *Rid of My Disgrace: Hope and Healing for Victims of Sexual Assault* (Wheaton, IL: Crossway, 2011), 31–33.

Children need to know about private parts.

One in **four women** and **one** in **six men** have been or will be sexually assaulted in their lifetime.

GOD SAW EVERYTHING HE HAD MADE. AND IT WAS VERY GOOD.

GENESIS 1:31

Mom said, "Kayla, God made everything and called it good.

Who made you?"

"God made me," said Kayla.

"When God made people he called it very good," said Mom.

"David, what else did God make?" asked Dad.

David said,

"GOD MADE ALL THINGS."

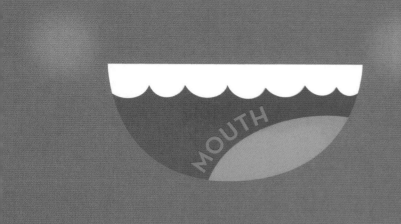

MOUTH

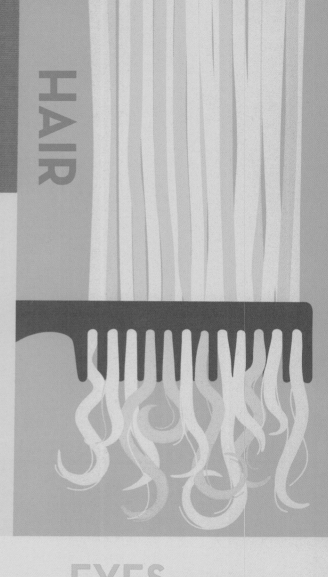

HAIR

HOW YOU MADE ME IS AMAZING AND WONDERFUL. I PRAISE YOU FOR THAT. WHAT YOU HAVE DONE IS WONDERFUL. I KNOW THAT VERY WELL.

PSALM 139:14

EYES

Mom said, "God made your eyes, your hair, your nose, your ears, your mouth, your teeth. God made all of your body parts."

Jumping up, Kayla said, "God made my legs and feet and toes, too."

Smiling, Dad said, "Yes, you are right, Kayla. From your head to your toes—everything about you is special to God! We can thank God that he made us in such a special and wonderful way."

NOSE

ARMS

"God made every part of your body and God called every part of your body good. Some parts of your body are for sharing and some parts are not for sharing," said Dad.

"I can share a **hug** or a **kiss** if I want. Right?" asked Kayla.

David added, "I can share a

high five

or a handshake if I want."

Mom said,
"And if you don't want to be **hugged**

or

kissed or give a **high five**

or a

handshake,

just say,

No,
thank you.

"It's **OK** to say no
because we don't always want to be touched
even if it's by someone you LOVE.
If the person doesn't listen to you,
ask for help right away."

David said, "I can tell you or Daddy or my teacher or the doctor."

DADDY   MOMMY   TEACHER   DOCTOR

"That's right, David."

Mom said, "God made **every part** of your body,
and every part of your body is good.
Some parts of your body are not for sharing;
these are called your private parts.

"**Private parts** are the parts covered by your underwear
or bathing suit and should not be touched by other people.
These include your penis, vagina, bottom, and breasts.

"Sometimes you need help going to the bathroom or taking a bath and we help you.

"And sometimes the doctor checks your body parts to make sure you are healthy. Parents and doctors use safe and healthy touches to keep kids healthy and strong.

If you aren't sure if it is a safe and healthy touch, you can always ask. Touches are never secret.

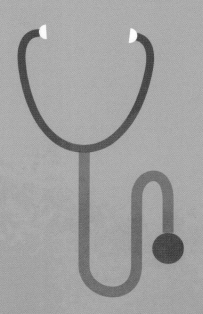

"Everyone's body has private parts. Private parts are not for sharing and should be kept private. It is important to ask for help if someone shares or shows their private parts or asks you to share or show yours.

"Also, there are no such things as games that involve private parts. There are no prizes, treats, or rewards for showing or touching private parts."

 EYES

 TUMMY

 HEART

Dad said, 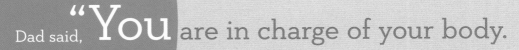"**You** are in charge of your body.

You can say **Stop**, **All done**, or **No more** if you don't want to be touched. A lot of the time you like to be hugged, snuggled, tickled, and kissed, but sometimes you don't and **that's OK**.

"Let me know if anyone—a family member, a friend, or anyone else—touches you or talks to you in a way that makes you feel uncomfortable.

"And if anyone touches you anywhere on your body (private parts or anywhere else) and it makes you feel

weird, uncomfortable, scared, angry, or sad, you can say **No** and go ask for help right away."

"You mean even if someone touches my leg or back or face and I don't want them to?" David asked.

"Yes, David. That's exactly right," Mom said.
"If you are confused about the touching,
you can say No and go get help right away.
Find Daddy or me and tell us about it."

David said, "But what if you or Daddy or my teacher are too busy to talk?"

"It is very important to keep asking for help until someone listens," Mom said. "You are very special and deserve to be safe. Let's think of people who can help you if you need it.

"Who makes you feel

SAFE

and

STRONG?"

NOTE FOR PARENT:

Brainstorm with your child a list of people to help them feel safe.

"What do you know about

SECRETS?"

Dad asked.

David said, "People tell secrets when they don't want other people to know things."

"That's right," Dad said. "And we don't keep secrets because we don't have anything to hide from each other. If anyone ever tells you to keep a secret from Mommy or me, tell us right away.

You **won't** get into trouble for telling us."

"What do you know about
SURPRISES?"
Mom asked.

Kayla said, "We surprised
Daddy with a present on his
birthday!"

"Surprises are fun and make
people happy. **Secrets are different from surprises.** Secrets are
not nice, they can make people feel confused or sad," said Mom.

"**Thank you** for keeping us safe,"

said Kayla. "I'm really glad that God made you and Daddy and David and me."

Smiling, Dad said, "Kayla and David, **I'm so glad that God made you and gave you to us.** God loves us so much and cares about our safety. That is why we talk about our bodies so we can help keep each other safe."

THE LORD GIVES ME STRENGTH. HE IS LIKE A SHIELD THAT KEEPS ME SAFE. MY HEART TRUSTS IN HIM, AND HE HELPS ME.

PSALM 28:7

9 Ways to Protect Your Children from Sexual Abuse

1. Explain to your child that God made their body.
An explanation can look something like, "Every part of your body is good, and some parts of your body are private."

2. Teach proper names of private body parts.
It might be uncomfortable at first, but use the proper names of body parts. Children need to know the proper names for their genitals. This knowledge gives children correct language for understanding their bodies, for asking questions that need to be asked, and for telling about any behavior that could lead to sexual abuse.

Clearly identify for your child which parts of their anatomy are private. Explain to your child that "some places on your body should never be touched by other people—except when you need help in the bathroom, or are getting dressed, or when you go to the doctor." You can do this with young children during bath time or have your child dress in a bathing suit and show them that all areas covered by a bathing suit are "private." The bathing suit analogy can be a bit misleading because it fails to mention that other parts of the body can be touched inappropriately (like mouth, legs, neck, arms), but it is a good start for little ones to understand the concept of private parts.

3. Invite your child's communication.
Let your child know they can tell you if anyone touches them in the private areas or in any way that makes them feel uncomfortable (even areas not covered by the bathing suit)—no matter who the person is or what the person says to them. Assure your child they will not be in trouble if they tell you they've been touched inappropriately—rather, you will be proud of them for telling you and will help them through the situation.

4. Talk about touches.
Be clear with adults and children about the difference between touch that is OK and touch that is inappropriate. To your child say something like: "Most of the time you like to be hugged, snuggled, tickled, and kissed, but sometimes you don't and that's OK. Let me know if anyone—family member, friend, or anyone else—touches you or talks to you in a way that makes you feel uncomfortable."

Teach little ones how to say "Stop," "All done," and "No more." You can reiterate this by stopping immediately when your child expresses that they are all done with the hugging or tickling. Your reaction is noteworthy for them as it demonstrates they have control over their bodies and desires.

If there are extended family members who may have a hard time understanding your family boundaries, you can explain that you are helping your children understand their ability to say no to unwanted touch, which will help them if anyone ever tries to hurt them. For example, if your child does not want to kiss Grandpa, let them give a high five or handshake instead.

5. Don't ask your child to maintain your emotions.
Without thinking, we sometimes ask a child something along the lines of, "I'm sad, can I have a hug?" While this may be innocent in intent, it sets the child up to feel responsible for your emotions and state of being: "Mom is sad . . . I need to cheer her up." If someone wanted to abuse a child, they might use similar language to have the child "help" them feel better; and the child might rationalize it as acceptable if this is something they do innocently with you.

6. Throw out the word "secret."
Explain the difference between a secret and a surprise. Surprises are joyful and generate excitement, because in just a little while something will be unveiled that will bring great delight. Secrets, in contrast, cause isolation and exclusion. When it becomes customary to keep secrets with just one individual, children are more susceptible to abuse. Perpetrators frequently ask their victims to keep things secret just between them.

7. Clarify rules for playing "doctor."
Playing doctor can turn body parts into a game. If children want to play doctor, you can redirect this game by suggesting using dolls and stuffed animals as patients instead of their own body. This way they can still use their doctor tools, but to fix and take care of their toys. It may take some time for them to make the shift, but just remind them gently that we don't play games, like doctor, with our bodies. If you find your child exploring his or her own body with another child, calmly address the situation and set clear boundaries by saying, "It looks like you and your friend are comparing your bodies. Put on your clothes. And remember, even though it feels good to take our clothes off, we keep our clothes on when playing." [Dialogue from: Stop It Now! tip sheet "Talking to Children and Teens" (http://www.stopitnow.org/talking_to_kids).]

8. Identify whom to trust.
Talk with your kids about whom you and they trust. Then give them permission to talk with these trustworthy adults whenever they feel scared, uncomfortable, or confused about someone's behavior toward them.

9. Report suspected abuse immediately.
You've read these steps, now consider yourself an advocate against childhood sexual abuse. Report anything you know or suspect might be sexual abuse. If you don't, it's possible no one else will.

This section summarizes some portions from two Stop It Now! tip sheets: "Don't Wait: Everyday Actions to Keep Kids Safe" (http://www.stopitnow.org/dont_wait_everyday_prevention) and "Talking to Children and Teens" (http://www.stopitnow.org/talking_to_kids).

JUSTICE
MERCY
COMPASSION

The mission of GRACE is to empower the Christian community through education and training to recognize, prevent, and respond to child abuse. GRACE exists to equip and assist faith communities to mirror God's justice, mercy, and compassion for children and abuse survivors of all ages. GRACE is made up of highly trained and experienced multi-disciplined professionals and provides abuse prevention training, abuse response assistance, consultations, and independent investigations.

GRACE
Godly Response to Abuse
in the Christian Environment

netgrace.org